THE STUDY GROUP:
A HANDBOOK FOR
REVOLUTIONARIES

THE STUDY GROUP

J. Katsfoter

Unity-Struggle-Unity Press

2023

ISBN: 978-1-312-56490-9

Table of Contents

Introduction: Why Study Groups?

From the beginning, the primary kernel of socialist organization has always been the study group or reading circle. Before there were socialist parties, before there were Communist parties, there were study groups and reading circles. These developed and differentiated into organs and organizations of action. The radical press has always been critical to this crystallization in every period.

The question of organization is the primary one confronting the Communist movement in the U.S. Empire and its junior partner in imperialism, Canada. How are we to organize? How are we to recover from the disastrous effects of the state attacks of the 1960s and 70s? How can we defeat the disorganization that has demobilized and debilitated our movement?

The first task of the Communist, in the era of disorganization, is to combat eclecticism. What do we mean by this? Simply: in the absence of the party, in the absence of a militant; developed; revolutionary; and, above all, correct and scientific centralized party school, the movement degrades, decays, and is adulterated with incorrect, adventurist, or opportunist notions.

To put it very simply — the first task of the Communist movement is to eliminate underdevelopment. This can be done on an individual basis by self-taught and dedicated students of history, theory, and Communism. This can not be done on a systemic basis without organization. Part of the task of eliminating underdevelopment is the reproduction of new, developed, militant Communists. A movement that cannot maintain and replicate its dedicated membership is destined to perish. Individual members falling victim to ccircumstance should never damage the overall level of development of an advanced Communist organization.

Therefore, it is no idle fancy that we suggest the study group — the reading circle — as the focus of local work. The study group has historically been the way in which socialists educate themselves and each other. This is the methodology of early socialist development. We must consider ourselves to be in such a phase. We do not suggest the study group because it is simple or because it is the topic which we chose from a hat, but because it is a foundational type of primary Communist organization.

To that end, we must speak briefly of **primary organizations**. A primary organization, fully developed, is a local, cellular part of a Bolshevized party. (For more on this term, please see the USU Handbook for Revolutionaries on Bolshevization by Comrade Mazal). It is an organization with a discrete area of responsibility; historically, this would be a geographical or workplace distinction. Primary organizations might be based in a town, city, or other locality; they might be based on a factory or a type of worker in an area. **We believe that the primary organization that is most important to form is the Communist school, the social study group.** As the engine drivintg the education of Communists, the school empowers the creation and development of all future organs. Study and development cannot occur in isolation, it must be performed in concert with others. Study groups should evolve from the voluntarist "circle" principle toward the disciplined "organization" principle — that is, from a simple association of people who are reading together into a real formal organization with rules and discrete membership.

We hope this guide will allow Communists all over the imperial U.S. and its dependencies to form study group organizations that will grow into real, local primary organizations. As they grow and maintain their capacity to produce new militants, they should differentiate and create new organs — internal to themselves, rather than whole new organizations — to handle new tasks and responsibilities. In time, these study groups will have the capacity to develop from primary organizations into regional coordinating organs. At some indefinite time in the future, all of these may be organized into the reconstituted vanguard.

It is worth more clearly drawing the distinction between the mass organization and the primary organization.

Mass organizations are not composed solely of Communists and may not be explicitly Communist at all — in fact, they likely aren't. Communists generally enter into mass organizations to help raise the class-consciousness of their membership and to identify and develop possible Communists within their ranks.

Primary organizations are those all-Communist organizations which are designed to have discrete areas of responsibility, as mentioned above.

There is a great deal of confusion and uncertainty surrounding the term "mass org" as it is used today. It may be that it is frequently used incorrectly. In our view, the state of the movement in the U.S. Empire (etc.) is, today, so anemic and divided, that there are few, if any, functioning primary organizations. In the ideal sense, such organizations would have a kind of geographic, local, mandate to oversee the Communists of a single area. They might have internal divisions for certain tasks. At some point, we expect them to report to a local coordinating organization: a committee of committees, as it were.

However, that is not the case today. Today, we must stress the importance of building primary organizations as study and reading groups. This will often take the form of a mixed-consciousness group. Why? Because we lack the number of trained, militant, devoted Communists to do otherwise. Thus, we may see the study group arising as a mass organization with Communist organizers and leadership.

It should become the goal of any such organization, as the handbook will later explain in detail, to concentrate in its central apparatus (its primary organization), a number of devoted, militant Communists. It is still possible for this primary organization to be involved in the running of a mass study group. That group would be much less strict than a Communist one (i.e. subject to democratic voting of non-Communists on what to read, etc.).

We hope, in essence, that local groups can start with a seed that then unfolds different branches and petals, with some branches remaining undivided until they are mature enough to stand on their own. We are speaking of a process that must occur over time: the sprouting up of subsidiary organizations, or the calving off of parts of an organization. This does not mean that any physical separation has to take place. Here we are speaking only metaphorically — organizationally. Indeed, these new petals and branches, flowerings and unfoldings, need not even take the form of separately organized bodies but may be (and most likely should be) the constituent parts of a fully-matured primary organization.

In this way, we believe it is possible to grow from two or three Communists into a thriving mass organization that eventually becomes a real primary organization; perhaps one that runs external mass organization study circles.

A note for the book worshippers

"Where did this idea of primary organizations come from? Surely you did not create it whole-cloth out of the ground!" Although I would strenuously argue that, even if we had merely, ourselves, been the first "discoverers" of the differentiation between primary organizations and the fully-constituted vanguard party, between party organizations and mass organizations, that it would not make it any less correct. The fact of the matter is that this comes not only from the study of modern conditions, but from historical study. For those of you, then, who cannot or will not act until you have consulted the hoary and ivy-covered tomes of our revolutionary past and found in them ample justification for an act, I present a very abbreviated history of this concept.

The Russian Social Democratic Labor Party (the RSDLP, which would eventually become the CPSU(B)), the world's first successful Communist revolutionaries and thus the baseline from which we adapt to account for our own conditions, was formed in the late 19th century only after decades of valiant but failed attempts at socialist organizing in the Tsarist Empire. Comrade Stalin writes:

In the decade of 1884-94 the Social-Democratic movement still existed in the form of small separate groups and circles which had no connections, or very scant connections, with the mass working-class movement....

In 1895 Lenin united all the Marxist worker's circles in St. Petersburg (there were already about twenty of them) into a single League of Struggle for the Emancipation of the Working Class.... Lenin proposed to pass from the propaganda of Marxism among the few politically advanced workers who gathered in the propaganda circles to political agitation among the broad masses of the working class on issues of the day....

In 1898 several of the Leagues of Struggle — those of St. Petersburg, Moscow, Kiev, and Ekaterinoslav — together with the Bund made the first attempt to unite and form a Social-Democratic party. For this purpose they summoned the First Congress of the RSDLP which was held in Minsk in March 1898.[1]

Lenin himself wrote,

When I say that the Party should be a sum (and not a mere arithmetical sum, but a complex) of organizations.... I thereby express clearly and precisely my wish, my demand, that the Party, as the vanguard of the class, should be as organized as possible, that the Party should admit to its ranks only such elements as lend themselves to at least a minimum of organization.[2]

In 1904, Lenin criticized the Second Party Congress of the RSDLP and wrote One Step Forward, Two Steps Back, where he clearly laid out the difference between a "mass" party and a vanguard party. This criticism was the result of a struggle between Lenin and Martov, the famous debate over "Paragraph 1" of the party rules. Martov's version read, "Party membership. 1) A member of the Russian Social-Democratic Labour Party is one who, accepting its programme, works actively to accomplish its aims under the control and direction of the organs of the party."

Lenin's reply? "My opponent... lumps together in the Party organized and unorganized elements, those who lend themselves to direction and those who do not, the advanced and the incorrigibly backward." In his notes, Lenin remarks that,

The word 'organization' is commonly employed in two senses, a broad and a narrow one. In the narrow sense it signifies an individual nucleus of collective people with at least a minimum degree of coherent form. In

1. J.V. Stalin, *History of the Communist Party of the Soviet Union - Bolshevik (Short Course)*, 18-19 (Pravda Media, 2016).
2. V.I. Lenin, *One Step Forward, Two Steps Back*, 1904

the broad sense, it signifies the sum of such nuclei united into a whole.

What was Lenin's Paragraph 1? That a member must not only accept the Party's Programme and give it financial support, but personally participate in the work of one of its organizations.

For those who continue to doubt that the RSDLP/CPSU(B) was organized into primary organizations and higher levels, we would instruct a brief course in the constitution of the Communist Party of China. This party has local primary organizations of party committees (existing at neighborhood level and even within landlord and property management organizations) elected by a local party congress.

If we are to have any hope of reconstituting the vanguard party in the U.S. Empire, we must strive to be at least as organized as the Russian Marxists of the 1880s!

Overview

This guide is divided into several sections. The first details how to agitate in your locality, how to locate other Communists or aspiring Communists, and how to begin integrating them into the core of a study group. It may be that these budding Communists are not developed enough to begin immediately interacting with the masses (as anticipated in this guide) and that they may require time to develop themselves before they form an organizing committee for any type of mass study group.

The second section details one possible manner of organization for the study group. These are organizational structures and methods of accounting for tasks, assignments, and labor.

The third section details running meetings; although this is specifically regarding the study group, it contains principles that are generally useful in holding any kind of meeting.

The last section contains sample reading lists, rules of order, and bylaws, which can be lifted almost wholesale for use.

Agitating for a Study Group

At this point, you have already decided that a study group is an appropriate vehicle for starting a local organization or helping to supplement already-existing local formations. Before you make final decisions about forms, reading lists, meeting rules, and so on, you will need to take a good, hard look at the local conditions. Only once you yourself have had a chance to mull over the general development and militancy in the area will you be able to make informed decisions about a study group.

Once you've got a general assessment, you will pick places to put up flyers or leave literature and individuals you already know to approach about joining the study group. You will have to make decisions about other tendencies and how you'll deal with them, and other decisions about which organizations you're a part of or otherwise adjacent to that you want to invite.

You'll want to decide whom you want in the study group and what general level of development you think they'll have. You'll also likely need a few other comrades to help you form an Organizing Committee. Additionally, you'll want to write or adopt some basic rules before you get underway. After all, hosting a study group can help you create and maintain organization by giving the participants an opportunity to be part of an organization that doesn't have immensely high stakes. Study groups can serve as "practice orgs," in a way.

What is a Study Group?

When approaching any task, we should have a firm notion of what it is we're doing, how it serves the advancement of the revolution, and what strategies we should use to make certain we're accomplishing our overall goals. You've already decided that a study group is the right form for approaching your local conditions. However, you should firmly keep in mind what exactly the study group is good for, how to arrange its formal structure to ensure you're driving at the correct tasks, and how you will differentiate the study group proper from the organization that is running the study group.

Generally, we have used the term "study group" interchangeably with "organization that is running a study group." In very simple or rudimentary formations, these two terms can continue to be used interchangeably because they will, in most cases, overlap entirely. However, there is a difference!

This guide will address both, and we will do our best to keep them distinct to make the strategy clear. The study group itself is a tool of political development and propaganda; the organization running the study group is a tool of organizing, that is, of arranging semi-permanent or permanent standing relationships and structures for making decisions. When running a study group according to this method, you will both be developing potential new Communists and cadre and helping to organize already-existing Communists into a formation capable of taking action.

If your resources are slim, you will likely begin organizing with 1-4 trained or semi-trained Communists. This will comprise your study group organization. These 1-4 trained or semi-trained Communists (whom we will call the "organizers") will facilitate the study group or groups themselves with any number of attendees. The primary goal of running the study sessions will be to develop attendees into organizers and bring them into your organization. Little by little, as the organization grows, it will develop specialized committees and organs for taking care of tasks. Once the organization reaches a certain minimum membership (perhaps 20-30 members), it need not confine itself to merely running study groups. It can become a real and coherent pre-party organization — that is: a Marxist-

Leninist Political Club.

It is vital that this "club" not act as a repository of hobbyists. It must be outward-looking, ever seeking to make contact with other local organizations — of all stripes, but most importantly, primary Communist organizations — across the U.S. Empire. This is why we so strenuously recommend the creation of a Committee of Correspondence (which we will expand on in Section III).

To be clear, then, we can differentiate these two concepts like this: the Study Group Organization and the Study Session. Study sessions don't really require formality when they're being held. Business meetings (that is, meetings to decide on matters of substance) of the Study Group Organization do. We will address this more fully in Section IV, Meetings, below.

The Social Investigation

Before you do anything else, you should conduct a little social investigation. This doesn't have to be exhaustive; this investigation aims to give you a firmer footing on which to decide certain foundational questions. You should consider the following things when preparing this investigation:

- The class composition of your area;
- The current degree and militancy of the struggle in your area;
- The most acute contradictions nearby;
- The number of Communists or pro-Communist elements in your immediate area;
- The political development and militancy of those elements;
- The number of anti-Communist elements in your immediate area;
- And, the danger and militancy of those elements.

How does one go about doing this? While this isn't a handbook on social investigation best practices, there are a few tools we can briefly discuss. You should also keep in mind that social investigations are normally undertaken by fully-formed organizations using their mass outreach arms. This is not that kind of complete social investigation. Rather, this is more of a quick and rough overview of regional and local issues using limited resources, most of which you should be able to find online.

First and foremost, research on the demographic makeup and income of your region will help you get an immediate handle on the major contradictions. This information is usually available through government census data and other aggregators. Often "demographics by income" will turn up useful maps and breakdowns. Although you won't be able to determine the actual class composition by the reported incomes, this will serve as a good thumbnail sketch.

Suppose you're in a cosmopolitan area. In that case, the concentration of demographics by national origin will immediately reveal the situation regarding national oppression. In rural areas, you'll be less likely to see this contradiction immediately through the lens of income and capitalist "demographics." Nevertheless, it's still a part of the investigation worth doing. It will often manifest in intensive agricultural labor in a rural area.

You can also "be amongst the people" and ask about their issues. This will generally require you to be plugged into another organization or be very adept at striking up conversations on the bus or other public transportation. These kinds of conversations will reveal the underlying contradictions that affect most of the people most of the time. Even if you are yourself subject to the pressures of very sharp or extreme contradictions, it can be useful (and often is) to conduct this kind of broader survey, even if it is informal. We should always remember that our work should be aimed at the broadest possible section of the working classes; there's a very human tendency to universalize our experiences and assume that everyone is experiencing the sharpening contradictions in the same way, especially within our own individual class, but any individualized experience runs the risk of being in some way exceptional — that is, out of the ordinary. It's important to understand that this also applies to individual anecdotes from those with whom you converse; this is not a comprehensive scientific study, but rather an initial probe to help guide your organizational trajectory.

When you are "amongst the people," you must listen to them! You must not lecture! The purpose of being amongst the people is to learn from them. You should ask them questions, listen to their answers, and record them. You can frame some preliminary or rudimentary bits of Communist theory, but do not attempt to transform what is an investigation into an opportunity to pontificate! We must never become vulgar proselytizers.

Class composition. Correctly identifying the class composition of the area will allow you to determine where and how best to agitate for your study group's formation. This should include a granular breakdown of local conditions — in college towns, you'll find many petit-bourgeois and bourgeois students; you may locate apartment complexes with low rents, where students with a predominately proletarian class background congregate; in agricultural communities, you are likely to find low-paid precarious laborers who are in the region temporarily and more long-term petit-bourgeois smallholders who have to supplement their agricultural income with second jobs; in cities with a functional industrial base, you'll find the proletariat dominates.

By comparing the class composition analysis with the analysis determining the sharpest points of location contradictions, you will find weak points and wedge issues that can mobilize sections of that class to attend a study session. This will also help you pick reading lists and decide on starting literature, and should give you a good idea of physical locations near the heart of the class struggle where you might be able to set up shop and hold your readings and study sessions.

Local struggle and local contradictions. These two elements intimately play into one another. Ideally, the local militancy of the various "left" movements (and in these, we should self-consciously include Social Democrats, Anarchists, and other "fellow travelers") should line up and be set to address the most intense or sharpest of local and empire-wide contradictions. In practice, however, without a guiding organization, this is rarely the case. More often, one will find a relatively disorganized degree of local struggle aimed at addressing "pet issues," or the issues which seem most important or are at the forefront of the consciousness of the small cliques leading these local organizations and formations.

To be clear: this is not debilitating, but it is not the way struggle, in best practices, would be run. It's valuable for the members of a study group to identify (or pre-identify) both the sharpness of the local contradictions and the development of the local struggle.

To identify the development of the local struggle, one must simply record the numerous "left" groups in the area, what struggles or issues they have made it known they are addressing or attempting to redress, the number of members in each (if known), and the degree of organization each of those groups possesses. It can be helpful (but is not necessary) to identify the general ideological tendencies professed by each group and the dominant ideological tendency actually expressed by each group.

Once you have done this, you can also draw up the list of local contradictions and identify which are the sharpest and most driving. If you come up with a match between an organization that is addressing the sharpest (or among the sharpest) of contradictions, it may be worthwhile to recruit for the study group among that organization; these people are at the forefront of the local struggle and providing them space and material to help develop will increase their effectiveness in combating the contradictions which plague the working masses.

If none of the groups are addressing what you have identified as a core contradiction, you can still recruit from among them; it may be that your recruiting tactics should include the organizations that may be amenable to further organizing or development to help steer them toward the most acute contradictions, or it may be that the inclusion of these elements can rectify your own analyses in the case that it is mistaken.

The main thing, of course, is that identifying these confluences will give you a good idea of how to configure your initial reading list or pool of potential reading material. For instance, if the local conditions reveal a major contradiction is in the incarceration of young Black and Latiné people, the reading list would be well-served to incorporate readings on the capitalist prison-industrial complex or even accounts written by Marxists incarcerated in the U.S. prison system (such as Assata Shakur's autobiography Assata or anything by George Jackson).

Communist/pro-Communist elements. Identifying Communist or pro-Communist formations aligns with identifying the militancy and development of the local struggle. This is where your nascent study group will try to identify friendly or potentially friendly formations. Here you can take the analysis you've already done on the local struggle and sort out the groups which you believe have the potential of being friendly, the conflicts you can foresee arising with them, and the ways in which those conflicts can be avoided. We generally refer to this process as identifying non-antagonistic contradictions and maneuvering those elements out of contradiction. For the current development of our movement, local organizations should be working toward unity on whatever basis is possible, particularly when your own study group is unformed or embryonic and will not have sufficient ground-support, membership, penetration, etc., to stand up to conflict, even over "principled" stands. This should not be taken as advocating for the abandonment of your principles but rather something more nuanced — the identification of your minimum points of unity and the imposition of those points in the way that is least likely to isolate you from the local movement.

What do we mean by this? Openly chauvinistic violations of the minimum commitments you've pledged your own principles to don't represent non-antagonistic contradictions but rather antagonistic ones. However, you should identify the farthest right your program or commitments extend, making every effort to encompass the most elements of the local movement you can. You should then go about identifying which organizations are in actual antagonistic contradiction with these commitments and which are not; not on the basis of something you heard about the organization on social media or something its all-empire organs have done or are doing, but rather on the basis of its local organization. The purpose of this distinction is that if an organization has an antagonistic contradiction with your program at an all-empire level but the local organs do not actively adhere to that program (are, perhaps, struggling against it), you may render them aid or even break them off of the chauvinistic all-empire group.

Drawing up points of unity is neither a simple nor easy task, especially if you are trying to start your study group on your own. We have provided a sample document that we believe represents the correct lines; however, we encourage you (and your comrades if you are forming this study group with other people) to review the program and make edits after consideration of your local conditions.

Anti-Communist elements. The last major consideration you should take is for fascist and other anti-Communist organizations that might disrupt your study sessions. This can be addressed in much the same way as your assessment of local struggle and the forces behind it. Obviously, the police are ever-present and semi-hostile, but at the present moment, it is possible to mostly avoid police scrutiny even when discussing revolutionary politics, so long as the organization is "polite" and maintains at least a few white men to handle police interaction.

A note about accessibility

Obviously, your meetings should be accessible to the widest selection of people who might want to attend. This may require running a supplemental Discord server or other such method of meeting — particularly in rural areas, where population is very dispersed.

It should be noted that there is no perfect substitute for in-person meetings. There is simply no way to treat online meetings with an equivalent degree of formality, decorum, and organizational precision. You will always suffer from information loss in an online setting!

After determining the level of danger, the size and disposition of anti-Communists, etc., this will help to inform whether the meetings of the study group should be held openly and in public (which is optimal) or whether the danger requires that they be held covertly and/or privately.

Gathering Membership

Before you begin gathering attendees, you should start by attempting to gather organizers. You can advertise for organizers the same way you advertise for attendees, but it is very important that you trust the other organizers. They must be developed Marxist-Leninists capable of sustaining long-term work. For that reason, **we recommend that you identify at least 2-4 other Marxist-Leninists you know and trust implicitly to help you in this process.** Even before you begin step one, it would be good to read this manual with these other organizers. Once you have gathered a core of organizers (who will make up the organizing body), you should move on to advertising for attendees.

Getting people to join a study group is a classic application of the propagandist's art of agitation. Because you will have your analysis from the general social investigation, you will be able to form a clear plan of whom you will target and then follow that up with how you will target them. This will likely include members of the organizations you identified above, particularly those which are actually or nominally Marxist-Leninist and those which are most developed or most central to the struggle in the region. You will also likely want to mark for the study group those class-fractions that are suffering under the most acute contradictions, local downwardly-mobile petit-bourgeoisie and petit-bourgeois students, and potentially petit-bourgeois intellectuals in your locality.

If the level of anti-Communist danger is low, your recruitment methods can be very unrestrained. That is, you can openly post flyers, leave stacks of them in local cafes, request special editions of the *Red Clarion* (or other material) directly from our press, complete with advertisements for your study group incorporated on their front pages. If you have access to public transport or the workplaces of the class-fractions that you've defined or identified as the most revolutionary (that is, are at the crux of most acute class contradictions), these are both optimal places.

Additionally, depending on how willing you are to be

publicly exposed as a Communist, there are benefits to posting advertisements for the study group on local "left" Facebook groups, in local community organizing centers, and so forth. In major urban areas, Twitter can also be a valuable resource, whereas — in lower population or more rural regions, Twitter is unlikely to have the kind of local exposure needed to reach members.

Roughly, we can say the following physical locations are useful to canvas or drop advertisements when anti-Communist agitation is low:

- Cafes and coffee shops,
- Bookstores, particularly independent bookstores,
- Public places in your workplace (bulletin boards, etc.) as long as this won't be dangerous to you,
- Local community centers,
- Meetings of progressively-oriented groups (Black Student Unions, LGBT clubs, Muslim Student Associations, etc.),
- Student dormitories,
- Bus stations and public transportation hubs such as subways,
- Friendly churches and houses of worship such as temples, mosques, etc. (always ask permission here first),
- Libraries,
- Lampposts and other infrastructure in public,
- And anywhere else you can think of that would reach the radicals and semi-radicals you're looking for, which might include departmental desks in local colleges, etc.

If anti-Communism is rampant, you'll need to be much more careful about how you hand out flyers, where you post them, and what kinds of contact information you make available. You should not post your private phone number or email address publicly! An anonymized protonmail email address or a Google voice number are both good ways to avoid circulating your information in public as a Communist. No matter what, however, you should have a minimum of the following information displayed prominently on your study group flyers:

- Date and time of the first or next meeting
- Location of the meeting
- An email address or phone number to correspond with (you can use protonmail if you're worried about being connected to the project by dangerous people)
- A description of the study group ideology (i.e., anticapitalist, Marxist, etc.) in non-jargon terms

When designing these posters or flyers, you can now make use of the class analysis you've already done. They can target the contradictions you've identified as the most acute and hold out the offer for answers on how to address those pressing issues — and how to organize to realize those answers in a real, material way. This will help burgeoning radical anticapitalists connect to the material and give them a reason to reach out. The abstract notion of "study" doesn't necessarily scream "revolutionary action." It can be hard to connect this (necessary) aspect of political development with revolution, so it helps to focus directly on the manifestations of the contradictions of capitalism that people in the area see and experience firsthand on a weekly or day-to-day basis.

You should also plan to agitate face-to-face with people that you already know. With already-committed Communists, this kind of agitation can be as simple as "don't you want to join my study group?" When dealing with those with no Marxist training, those who are merely spontaneous anti-capitalists, this becomes a lot harder. Firstly, you have to recognize that, unless you're practiced at this kind of thing, it's likely going to feel embarrassing. Spontaneous anti-capitalists generally have to be asked repeatedly to join study groups or get involved with actions. That isn't to say that you should harass these people, but if they were ready to join a study group at the drop of a hat, they'd be almost ready to become autodidacts and begin their radical journey with or without your assistance. The number of people in that position is very small and will be the exception among the "awakening" people rather than the rule.

How to Handle Other Tendencies

One of the most common questions we've gotten when it comes to study groups (or any groups or coalitions that require some level of unity among various "kinds" of leftists and fellow travelers) is "how do you handle people who have different ideological tendencies?" The reason the question gets asked so often is due to the incredible rancor between tendencies over what, to most outsiders, appear to be very minor differences.

The advice here generally applies across other methods and locales of organizing as well — that is: to determine whether or not these individuals with other ideological commitments can agree to the minimum commitments of your own organizational program. If you're having trouble identifying a minimum ideological commitment, you should probably review the relevant section of USU's Constructive Struggle. If so, you can work with them and, indeed, they can join the main body of your organization. As you'll see further on, they may not be eligible for membership to the Selection Committee or whatever control system you create, but simply by working together, you can begin to develop a rapport and strengthen the (currently fragile) fabric of "leftist" networks in the United States Empire. Even if you eventually part ways, you will at least have managed to develop working relationships.

Obviously, this does not apply if the other tendencies

profess to be willing to work along the lines the study group has outlined but then manifestly fails to work along these lines. Constant disruption, bad-faith readings, and so forth will necessitate intervention either from you personally, the Selection Committee, or whatever other executive body your group has agreed upon (or that you have provided as the initial form).

Who Do You Want?

Everyone and anyone who can agree to abide by the rules, who doesn't exhibit wrecker or counter-revolutionary behavior or extreme uncorrectable chauvinism! Of course, the question becomes how to recruit this fantastic person we've created in our minds as the ideal target. The real trick isn't how to identify and recruit this one type of person alone, but rather to design and execute an atmosphere in which this type of person recruits themselves and the other, wrecker or dangerous types, can be weeded out.

The question about quality is not, then, a question about "who to recruit." So what is this section about? It's about ensuring your study group recruits broadly and among those suffering the most acute effects of capitalist contradictions while also maximizing the amount of time and energy that can be devoted to study and future organizing. What exactly do we mean by this? Simply, those most acutely affected by capitalism are those with the least amount of free time and energy to study its overthrow. That is to say, these two elements are in contradiction. This is not a contradiction that can be resolved, but rather an equilibrium that must be navigated, and not only through recruitment but through other structural corrections — for example, those who are suffering under the very acute contradictions of Capital should be able to rely on the study group to help alleviate those contradictions and permit them to devote time and energy to study. This is, of course, collective support — mutual aid, in the real sense of the term (rather than the bowdlerized sense that's often thrown around on the internet to describe red/black charity or Red Aid).

So who should you be recruiting, then? You should be targeting your recruitment efforts in two broad swathes of the population: the immiserated and the intellectual strata. You're going to be fusing together intellectuals from the petit-bourgeoisie, the bourgeoisie, and the proletarian classes into a single group of intellectuals who, regardless of their class-origins, have the class-ideology of the proletariat and, most importantly, have the class-allegiance of the proletariat.

Critically, however, you do not want to mix people at all different levels of advancement. This is a way to immediately burn out and turn off newer Communists or anti-capitalists. You cannot correct all errors at the beginning. The study group is a journey through gradients of correctness, which you must inculcate. So, if you are going to add a number of highly-developed people to a group full of new Communists, you must ensure that they have mastered the very difficult art of shutting the fuck up.

In fact, the Communist Party of China made it a rule to group people of like development, a few more advanced, a few less advanced, into study groups so they could struggle through the difficult questions together. If you are very developed or you are bringing in members who are very developed, you should be aware of this dynamic. Don't dominate the meetings by lecturing! This will be addressed further below, under "The Meeting."

Putting aside all sarcasm, who should you be attempting to recruit, in general? You should first and foremost try to build up the core of the study group by bringing on board as many left-leaning people you have personal relationships with; the optimal study group member is a new or learning Communist that you know well and who respects you. Whether these are co-workers, family members, or members of a radical organization isn't that important (again, unless you put yourself at risk by outing your ideological positions with, for instance, your family or your workplace). Once things are stable and the study group has been officially founded, established a semi-permanent home, and found its feet, you should expand this group to include strangers of various kinds, particularly those in the previously-identified most-affected classes.

Starting an Organizing Committee

The Organizing Committee will comprise the people you've invited to become organizers of the study group organization. You'll eventually become the study group's "organizer membership" or deciding body (it need not be named that; it can be called anything). The Organizing Committee should agree to adopt bylaws and rules (we have included samples) that allow it to become the organizing membership and direct the study group itself.

The Executive Committee is the heart of the study group organization; it serves as the guiding executive body of the organization and is the organization-in-embryo for those other groups and formations that eventually grow out of the study group. What is the Executive Committee? At that, what is a committee? We use this term in common parlance quite often without being aware of the semi-technical definition of the term. Still, it's important to understand how organizations function.

Committees are subdivisions of larger bodies that are given a specific set of responsibilities and commensurate powers to fulfill those responsibilities. Large meetings of hundreds and even thousands of delegates are unwieldy; it can take a long time for topics to be discussed, debated, and resolved. For this reason, the larger group assigns tasks (particularly the creation of reports and draft resolutions) to committees so these committees can discuss, debate, and write up recommendations to return to the larger deliberative body.

In the instance of the study group, the Executive Committee is a form that allows us to ensure that the study group continues to serve the purpose for which it was created and doesn't simply become a hobby. The Executive Committee maintains group cohesion, institutional memory, and direction between its meetings.

For this reason, this Committee should be composed of comrades that are highly developed Marxist-Leninists, preferably those you would classify as "cadre" — that is, who have a very high degree of militancy and political education and who are willing to make personal sacrifices for the sake of the organization, show up to most if not all organizational events, attend most if not all committee meetings, etc.

Even as few as two people can compose an Executive Committee (and, if you really can't find anyone else, even as few as one person can compose the "committee," although at that point, it wouldn't make sense to call it a committee or even formalize this relationship to the wider study group). You should implicitly trust the judgment of other comrades on the Executive Committee and approach them before you hold your first study group session. Indeed, forming the Executive Committee will serve as part of the planning process.

Organization

As we have hinted above, the organization of your study group will help determine whether or not it fulfills its dual purpose of developing new Communists into more militant, educated, and prepared agents of the Revolution and of organizing these new Communists into a form that can persist over time, make decisions; eventually transforming into a local Marxist-Leninist organization capable of entering into the field of revolutionary organizing and agitation.

While the general membership of the study group may appear to be the most obvious division of its organization, there is actually something that must precede this gathering of a general body: the Organizing Committee. This is the group that initially gathers prior to the creation of the study group to prepare the plan for how the study group will be executed. It should also draft the initial reading lists and choose or write study guides. It may be involved in the drafting or adoption of some draft rules of order and a draft set of points of unity. These will later be presented to the general membership for ratification, but generally only once the Executive Committee determines that the general membership is developed enough and has sufficient background to make an informed and knowing decision.

Other committees should be developed as the study group grows and its wider membership becomes more differentiated and developed. The initial committees will likely include a Reporting Committee, a Recruitment or Membership Committee, and a Scheduling Committee.

In essence, then, we should anticipate the following:

- An Organizing Committee — this group will meet before the study group is officially constituted. Its membership (probably between 1-5 people) will conduct and discuss their social investigation, adopt rules of order (or not), determine who to invite, draft an initial reading list, select or write study guides, draft a list of ideological commitments (that is, a program), and then self-dissolve, likely into the Executive Committee.

- The Executive Committee — membership of this committee will likely be selected by the Organizing Committee prior to its self-dissolution (probably every member of the Organizing Committee) and should remain closed until the general membership is developed sufficiently to have an informed and knowing say in choosing its members. The Executive Committee should curate the list of readings and present them to the general membership for a decision on what should be read next; it should make all or most inter-meeting decisions, and it should arrogate all the other committees' jobs to itself until there are sufficient people to staff them.

- A Reporting Committee — after the study group becomes sufficiently well-grounded and organized, it can be helpful to form a Reporting Committee that will assign investigations and reports to individual members. These reports can include "investigate this contradiction and report on the results at our next meeting," or asking members to pre-read certain books and submit recommendations to the Executive Committee.

- A Membership Committee — this committee generally oversees maintaining membership, working to increase membership, and may also be tasked with approving the developed members as they reach certain milestones, keeping track of membership lists, and even deciding when various members are developed enough to begin serving on various committees. Initially, this task will likely fall to the Executive Committee (the former Organizing Committee). The Membership Committee can also be tasked with designing the course of study for candidate members and interviewing these candidates to ensure they meet a minimum level of development, as is done in the Connecticut Radical Reading Group.

- A Scheduling Committee — may be tasked with coordinating everyone's schedules, finding and maintaining a place to meet, and even scheduling special events and one-off meetings.
- A Study Guide Committee — which can prepare study guides under the direction of the Executive Committee.
- A Treasury Committee — which maintains the books and funds of the study group organization.

A Note About Structure

It is imperative that the final shape of the organization give way to a democratically governed one. If you are seeking to form a *mass organization*, then the general mass membership would elect the executive committee of your study group. If you are trying to build a *primary Communist organization*, there are several options.

In my experience, the way to do this that works most effectively is to begin as a mass organization with a graduating process that separates *attendees* from *members*. As your mass, advanced worker attendees become more dedicated Marxists, they can graduate into leadership/general membership.

You should never ask people to pay dues and give required assignments to people who have no say in the direction or organization of the study group.

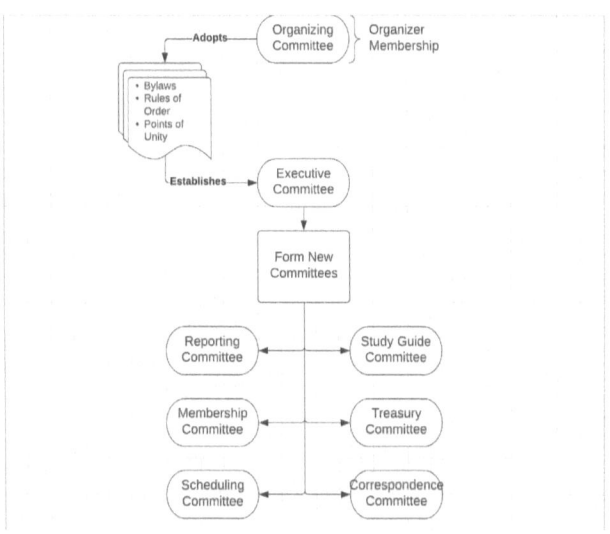

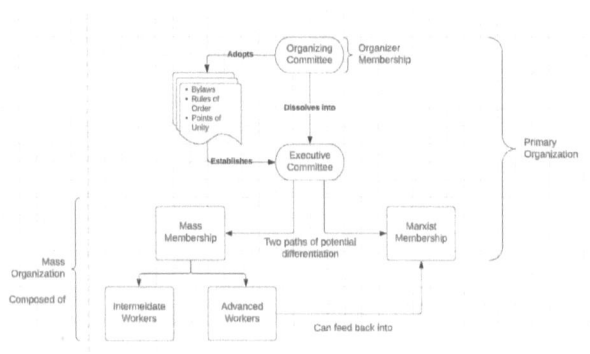

- A Committee of Correspondence, which is responsible for communicating with other groups and organizations across the U.S. Empire.

Other kinds of committees may be formed as the study group organization grows. As committees are formed, it should always be kept in mind that you don't want to overburden your membership. Try to keep people who are very busy in their personal lives from joining very active committees and try to keep people from joining more than two committees.

Early in the development of the study group organization, the jobs of these secondary committees may be devolved to individual officers (a Treasurer, a Scheduling and Membership Officer, etc.).

Standing outside these committees is the general membership. As we mentioned above, the organization's

A Note About Dues

Our sample bylaws include a provision that requires members to pay $20 per month in dues. There are many reasons for this — paying dues into the study group/organization, even when they're purely nominal, has a psychological grounding effect and tends to foster a sense of togetherness and commitment from those who pay it. A simple, low-cost dues amount can be used as a benchmark to establish a sliding scale or request donations from those who can afford it. The payment of dues can help the more well-situated members care for the needs of the less-well situated and make it more comfortable to meet in public (For instance, the society's funds can be used to ensure no one goes hungry if you're in a cafe), and serve as the basis from which to branch out and begin other projects.

general membership is divided into the organizers and attendees. Attendees come to study sessions; organizers run the study group.

Whether and how the study group differentiates and becomes more complex is ultimately something to be decided in concert between the participants and the initial organizers according to the needs, development speed, and capacity of the study group and the local conditions on the ground.

The Meeting

Study group meetings are different in a lot of important ways from the meetings of most other formal societies. First and foremost, they are generally very informal and should represent a safe and productive space for debate and discussion.

The primary thing about the study group meeting is to discuss the material. Everything else is secondary, including elevating organization through running the formal parts of a meeting and making more formal decisions. That is to say, in order to encourage development and growth of political education, it may be necessary to sacrifice some degree of militancy. Those in attendance should feel comfortable having wide-ranging discussions; should not feel rushed or hurried; and should certainly not feel constrained by the presence of more developed or "correct" people, which is the number one inhibitor to group learning in the U.S. anti-capitalist left today.

Meetings should start at a regular time. It's a good habit to begin the meeting at the same regular time every session to encourage consistency. If you're the only person in attendance, it's hard to "begin," but even keeping minutes and recording the time that people arrive if they come after the set starting time can instill some minimal sense of militancy and necessity for consistent attendance. Of course, again, you don't want to scare potential comrades off by stressing this point too much.

If your meetings are not yet highly organized, you can go straight into the discussion period. If you've been holding meetings for some time or you're dealing with a more militant or developed membership, you should start your meetings with business. Business meetings should be formal when your organization is prepared for it. Generally, groups with 2-3 people don't need any level of formality. Groups with 4-6 people require a minimal level of formality.

It is at the mark of 6-10+ that you really want to institute rules of order, formal motions, etc. Remember, part of this process is training the membership in being organized.

With a highly-militant and prepared study group, you can begin the meeting with a formal call to order, ask for business, present an agenda for the "business" section of the meeting, and generally proceed like any other organized society. In intermediate groups, you're better served by dividing the meeting into an informal business session and study portion, the business portion of which should last no more than 15 minutes. Business can and should include discussions of further formalizing the study group in small steps.

Once you deal with business matters (discussion of new points of unity, meeting place changes, changes to standard meeting times, discussion of potential actions, etc.), you should move on to the study portion of the meeting. A second business section at the conclusion of the meeting (addressing future reading and making sure everyone can attend the next meeting) helps keep cohesion by bookending the study portion.

Thus, a study group could hold meetings structured like this:

- **Call to Order** - *the sample rules of order are invoked at this point*
- **Pre-discussion business** (reports, points of unity, points of action, changing the meeting location on a permanent basis, alteration of the standard meeting times, bringing forward potential actions members might wish to attend in the upcoming weeks or months, electing a new Executive Committee or other officers)
- **Discussion** - *The rules of order are suspended at this point and the meeting proceeds informally until adjournment*

- **Post-discussion business** (one-time changes in the availability of members for the next meeting, one-time or short-term changes in meeting location, selecting new reading material)
- **Adjournment**

Discussions

Discussion of a text, local conditions, or theory is the heart of a study group. It should be prioritized above all other parts of the meeting, and maintaining a healthy and robust discussion portion will ensure the group will continue to develop and produce new, dedicated Communists who can enter the general movement or who can help transform the study group into the seed of a new local Communist organization.

The education of new Communists by the Alabama CPUSA in the 20s and 30s, the Communist Party of China, and the Bolsheviks all focused directly on the working classes: steel workers, rural proletarians, peasants, sharecroppers, etc. Common among these groups was a very low level of literacy. Thus, these meetings were usually conducted by cadre from the Party reading material aloud. Given the level of educational trauma associated with the bourgeois teaching methods of the U.S. Empire, many new Communists here have significant hurdles to overcome relating to dense or difficult economic material. For that reason, we have found it most helpful to emulate some of the techniques of our predecessors: those who are comfortable at our meetings take part in a round-circle, passing the reading from person to person section by section, which allows those who want to participate to feel a sense of investment in sharing the material. This also allows those who don't feel comfortable reading to remain comfortable while receiving the benefit of the read-aloud. It also relieves some of the pressure of reading between study sessions.

Reading Lists

The reading lists of your study group will vary based on the subjects that you have identified as being of particular importance, either to your locality (due to your analysis of local conditions) or to your membership, based on their input. It can be helpful to create "blocks" of material and divide your work into units. This would include things such as The National Question, Proletarian Feminism, etc.

The following reading list is the one in use at the Connecticut Radical Reading Group (CTRRG), a USU-founded group in Connecticut.

Political Economy and Socialism

- *Blood in My Eye*, George Jackson
- *Capital*, Karl Marx
- *Class Struggle*, Domenico Losurdo
- *Dialectical and Historical Materialism*, J.V. Stalin
- *Foundations of Leninism*, J.V. Stalin
- *The Fundamentals of Marxism-Leninism*, Otto Wille Kuusinen
- *Grundrisse*, Karl Marx
- *On Contradiction*, Mao Zedong
- *On the Origins of the Family, Private Property, and the State*, Friedrich Engels
- *Socialism, Utopian and Scientific*, Friedrich Engels
- *The State and Revolution*, V.I. Lenin
- *Wage Labour & Capital/Value, Price, and Profit*, Karl Marx
- *The Curriculum of the Basic Principles of Marxism-Leninism*, Luna Oi Translation

National Liberation

- *The Apocalypse of Settler-Colonialism*, Gerald Horne
- *Assata*, Assata Shakur
- *Black Reconstruction*, W.E.B. Du Bois

- *Blood of the Land*, Rex Wexler
- *Braiding Sweetgrass*, Robin Wall Kimmerer
- *Chicano Liberation and the Proletarian Revolution*, the August 29th Movement
- *Decolonial Marxism*, Walter Rodney
- *For a Revolutionary Position on the Negro Question*, Harry Haywood
- *Hammer & Hoe*, Robin D.G. Kelly
- *How Europe Underdeveloped Africa*, Walter Rodney
- *Imperialism: the Highest Stage of Capitalism*, V.I. Lenin
- *On the National Question*, J.V. Stalin
- *The Negro Nation*, Harry Haywood
- *The Open Veins of Latin America*, Eduardo Galleano
- *The Wretched of the Earth*, Frantz Fanon

Party Building

- *The 18th Brumaire*, Karl Marx
- *On Authority*, Friedrich Engels
- *Combat Liberalism*, Mao Zedong
- *Constructive Criticism*, Gracie Lyons
- *Constructive Struggle*, J. Katsfoter
- *The Dreyfus Affair*, Rosa Luxemburg
- *Fanshen*, William H. Hinton
- *How to Be A Good Communist*, Liu Shaoqi
- *One Step Forward, Two Steps Back*, V.I. Lenin
- *Reform or Revolution*, Rosa Luxemburg
- *Short Course History of the Communist Party of the Soviet Union (Bolshevik)*, J.V. Stalin
- *What is to be Done?*, V.I. Lenin

Sex Liberation

- *Caliban and the Witch*, Silvia Federici
- *Lenin on the Women's Question*, Clara Zetkin
- *Philosophical Trends in the Feminist Movement*, Anuradha Ghandy

- *The Straight Mind and Other Essays*, Monique Wittig

Others

- *Black Bolshevik*, Harry Haywood
- *Blackshirts and Reds*, Michael Parenti
- *Liberalism, a Counter History*, Domenico Losurdo
- *The Negro Nation*, Harry Haywood
- *Pedagogy of the Oppressed*, Paolo Friere
- *Stalin: History and Critique of a Black Legend*, Domenico Losurdo

Sample USU Rules of Order and Bylaws

Bylaws structure your study group and help everyone have the same expectation of how it will function and what its purpose and ambit are. You don't have to adopt bylaws, and some mass organizations are better off not having them, but if you're attempting to heighten the degree of organization in a group or to transform the simple study circle into a more robust study group, one that can itself become the core of a larger and more capable organization, bylaws are a good place to start. Sample bylaws follow this section.

Rules of order govern how you conduct meetings. For study groups, these can be rather loose — in fact, you can get by perfectly fine with no rules of order as long as you have ten or fewer people and you aren't trying to affect anything complicated during meetings. However, part of the benefit of organizing a study group is actually creating durable organizations; because the study group can be used as a launching-off point for a Marxist-Leninist organization and for actual practical efforts at revolutionary organizing above and beyond the creation of new revolutionaries, using the study group as an avenue to impart higher and higher degrees of organization.

To that end, even if the group doesn't strictly need a set of rules of order, they can be helpful. Their implementation can assist the transformation of the study group from an educational formation into a formation capable of action. In this section, we have included a sample set of rules of order that you can use as a benchmark, adopt wholesale, or completely ignore. It is important to note here that the study group does not contemplate strict democratic centralism as its main mode of operation.

Bylaws

Article I: Name.

The name of this society shall be [insert name here].

Article II: Object.

The object of this Study Group is to study and contribute to the field of Marxism-Leninism, as enumerated within the Points of Unity.

Article III: Members.

1. The general public, in the form of revolutionaries or fellow travelers, shall be encouraged to attend meetings of the society and participate in non-committee discussions; the society shall endeavor to hold its study groups open to the general public.

2. Any present shall be entitled to be heard at meetings of the general body or at any meeting of any study session or group so long as they agree to the above principles.

3. All attendees shall agree to abide by the Points of Unity and to do their best to uphold it.

4. The general, voting, membership shall be composed of the society's Organizers.

5. Attendees shall be encouraged to attend meetings for an extended period before they shall be considered for membership as Organizers.

6. Attendees shall be considered for membership as Organizers upon the motion of any Organizer and, upon a report from the Membership Committee shall be considered Candidate Organizers.

7. Candidate Organizers shall engage in a certain course of study that is selected by the Membership Committee.

8. Once a Candidate Organizer has completed the course of study, that Candidate shall be submitted before the Membership Committee for an interview.

The Membership Committee shall then produce a recommendation which is submitted to the following Business Meeting of the general membership.

9. Once a Candidate Organizer has been confirmed by the general membership, only a properly-authorized disciplinary procedure can remove that member.

10. Members shall treat each other and all attendees with comradely respect at all times, in or out of meetings and shall mediate all disagreements to the best of their capacity.

11. Attendees need not be themselves avowed Marxist-Leninists, but must be willing to study Marxist-Leninist revolutionary theory.

12. Members and attendees shall make efforts to attend as many meetings of the general body of the study group as they can.

13. Members must maintain an attendance of greater than 50 per-cent of scheduled Business Meetings in any given year to maintain good standing.

14. Membership dues are to be assessed at $20 per month, such dues being required for the maintenance of good standing. Upon a vote of good cause, dues requirements may be suspended on a case-by-case basis.

15. Members who are not in good standing may not vote on any study group business, but are entitled to be heard at meetings.

16. Any Organizer or Candidate Organizer wishing to resign from this organization shall submit their resignation in writing to the Membership Committee, who shall record it and act.

Article IV: Officers.

1. At each Quarterly Meeting, the general membership shall elect a President and a Chief Clerk.

2. These officers shall persist in their offices until the

following Quarterly Business Meeting.

3. The Chief Clerk shall record all minutes of Business Meetings during their term and, at the end of the meeting, ensure that they are available to all Organizers and Candidate Organizers.

4. The Chief Clerk shall also maintain the Society Archive and ensure that the minutes and reports from all committees are available upon request by any Organizer or Candidate Organizer.

Article V: Meetings.

1. This Society shall conduct regular meetings in person on the first Sunday of each month, normally at the hour of noon, and such meetings shall run until 2:30 PM EST or such other time as shall be decided. One meeting each quarter shall be designated to be the Quarterly Meeting.

2. The primary business of each regular meeting shall be to address readings, discuss problems of theory, and advance the understanding and knowledge of each member and prospective member.

3. The first order of business at each monthly, regular meeting shall be to elect members of the Executive Committee as provided for in Article VI below.

4. Special meetings may be called by a call for a meeting to all members of the Study Group [using the following method].

5. No special meeting shall be scheduled over the objection of any member in good standing.

6. Article VI: Executive Committee.

7. The Executive Committee shall maintain the list of potential readings, which may be supplemented at any time by suggestions from prospective members or members.

8. This committee shall administer the selection of readings, facilitate discussion on readings, prepare

or select study guides, and otherwise attend to the business of ensuring the development of each member and prospective member.

9. Upon formation of the Study Group, the currently-constituted Organizing Committee shall be dissolved and each member shall become a member of the Executive Committee.

10. Members of the Executive Committee shall be elected once each month by the members in good standing, at the regular meeting before other business has begun.

11. Only members in good standing shall be eligible to stand for election.

12. The Executive Committee shall have [number of Organizers] seats at its inception.

13. The Executive Committee shall maintain [number of Organizers] seats or one-fifth the total membership of this Study Group, whichever is larger.

14. The Executive Committee shall have the power to act as any of the Standing Committees which are not currently constituted.

Article VII: Committees.

1. Special committees may be formed by the membership at any meeting with a majority vote.

2. Standing committees may be formed by the membership at any meeting with a two-thirds majority vote.

3. All committees shall be delegated discrete powers and given defined functions, but no committees may bind the general membership.

4. All committees shall select a Clerk to maintain their minutes.

5. All committees shall record their minutes and submit them to the Study Group.

6. At the time of the adoption of these bylaws, standing

committees shall not be staffed and their functions shall be relegated to the Executive Committee or to Officers; they shall be constituted only once the Executive Committee or the general membership determines it necessary.

7. If the Society has fewer than 25 total Organizers, Standing Committee duties shall be relegated to individual officers instead.

8. The Membership Committee shall keep records of all prospective and current membership, the standing of each member, and shall maintain these records; the Membership Committee shall submit a recommendation to the general membership as to the fitness of each prospective member when that prospective member is put up for admission to the general membership.

9. The Reporting Committee shall maintain a list of topics, a library of reports, and shall assign topics for reporting to members in good standing.

10. The Scheduling Committee shall maintain a record of all members and prospective members schedules and assist in the scheduling of all special meetings.

11. The Treasury Committee shall maintain the books of account and shall be responsible to the general membership and the Executive Committee for the study group's funds; this committee shall produce its books at any meeting where they are requested.

12. The Committee of Correspondence shall maintain communications with other study groups and anti-capitalist organizations whose commitments are not in conflict with this Study Group's Points of Unity.

Article VIII: Authority and Points of Unity.

1. This study group derives its authority from past revolutionary theory and praxis of the past incomplete social revolutions and from its dedication

to total liberation for all.

2.   This study group adopts the Points of Unity appended to these bylaws.

3.   This study group adopts the rules of order appended to these bylaws.

Article IX: Amendment.

These bylaws may be amended at any standing meeting by a two-thirds majority vote.

Rules of Order

Rule 1. Call to Order

1.1. Meetings are formally begun by the call to order issued by the President.

Rule 2. Quorum

2.1. One half of members in good standing or, if there are fewer than 10 members, two members in good standing, shall constitute a quorum for doing business at all regularly scheduled meetings.

2.2. Quorum requirements may be set on an ad-hoc basis for special meetings if the notice of that meeting has been properly distributed in accordance with these rules.

Rule 3. Orders of the Day

3.1. All standing committees shall first present any reports or referrals.

3.2. All special committees shall then present any reports or referrals.

3.3. Individuals shall then present any reports.

3.4. The President shall then call for other business.

3.5. The President shall then publish any agenda, including the other business which has been added during the prior order.

3.6. Each agenda item shall be addressed in turn by the President. Formal rules for taking and holding the floor shall be recognized at this time.

3.7. After the Orders of the Day, the meeting shall proceed to the reading and discussion period, during which point the entire study group shall act as a committee of the whole.

Rule 4. Time Limits

4.1. Time limits for holding the floor shall apply only while rules 3.4, 3.5, and 3.6 are in force.

4.2. Each member and prospective member shall be permitted to hold the floor for a maximum of five minutes.

Sample USU Points of Unity

Article I. Ideology

Section 1. This Study Group [Ed: This can be replaced with the name of the study group] is dedicated to the study of Marxism-Leninism and the science of socialist revolution.

Section 2. Marxism-Leninism is a living body of revolutionary theory and method; it is the culmination of revolutionary experience from the whole history of the class struggle.

Section 3. This Study Group shall take ideological and practical guidance from the relevant experiences and contributions of revolutionaries from every land and region.

Article II. Self-Determination

Section 1. We agree that all peoples have the right to self-determination.

Section 2. The universal realization of that right within and without the existing U.S. empire and its junior partner Canada, that is, the decolonization of North America, is a precondition for a just society.

Section 3. The anti-colonial and national liberation struggles constitute a special stage of the social revolution.

Section 4. The struggle includes the liberation and self-emancipation of the Black nation of New Afrika, all pre-Colombian Indigenous peoples, and the U.S. Empire's colonial territories.

Article III. Sex Liberation

Section 1. This group shall study a revolutionary materialist feminist theory and work to enumerate and expand it.

Section 2. The materialist feminist theory shall be distinguished from the reformist and unscientific feminist trends by: (i) recognition of gendered oppression as structural and (ii) recognition of the failure of reforms to bring about true emancipation.

Section 3. This Group is committed to depatriarchalization, entailing the full legal emancipation and structural liberation of women, LGBT persons, and gender-variant persons, and all efforts will be taken to ensure this is practiced in the Group's organization.

Section 4. This Group shall vigorously defend the rights of women, LGBT persons, and gender-variant persons within its membership and shall endeavor to make study and work accessible and safe for such persons through a process of internal depatriarchalization.

Article IV. Disability Liberation

Section 1. This Study Group agrees that the abolition of disability as a social structure and for the liberation of disabled persons is a vital component of the social revolution.

Section 2. This Group shall ensure that disabled comrades and members are included and empowered to participate in all branches of the Group's work and study.

A Final Note

We at Unity–Struggle–Unity Press take very seriously our duty to be responsive to the real, practical experience of those revolutionaries and would-be revolutionaries who are making use of our handbooks. We encourage those who use them to give us feedback about their content and construction. Indeed, nothing could be better for the movement than for a continuous back-and-forth communication to spring up between organizations, circles, and groups pursuing the goal of Communism.

If you have criticisms of this handbook, if you merely wish to communicate with the editors and members of the Pressworker's Organization, to report on the ground conditions at your workplace or in your community, or even to write for our mass newspaper, the *Red Clarion* — please! Reach out to us!

We can be reached at:

USUEditorial@protonmail.com

Other Organizing Materials

If you are a member of a Communist organization, you will, sooner or later (and, let's be honest, likely sooner), need to engage in some kind of struggle, either internally or with another organization.

Constructive Struggle is available on Lulu

The ***Red Clarion***, our mass political newspaper, is available at

clarion.unity-struggle-unity.org

www.ingramcontent.com/pod-product-compliance
Lightning Source LLC
Chambersburg PA
CBHW020330290526
45785CB00007B/2995